but, you promised....

Erika Nicole

BookLeaf Publishing

India | USA | UK

Presentation by *BookLeaf Publishing*

Web: www.bookleafpub.com

E-mail: info@bookleafpub.com

ISBN: 9789363309258

First edition 2024

ACKNOWLEDGEMENT

To my support system —my family and friends who get it, and supports me unconditionally. Anyone who has ever vibed with my words. This book is for you. Your love, laughter, and late-night talks have been my inspiration and my anchor.

To those who've walked with me through the highs and lows, and to the new connections still waiting to be made—thanks for being part of this journey.

My heartfelt appreciation also goes to Book Leaf Publishing for bringing these poems to life.

Forever

How we were raised really determines our perspective of this seven letter word.
Just be sure yours matches the person you want to spend it with.

"A big picture"

2

As the truth unfolded, a new piece was to added to the puzzle, making the picture even clearer.

The End

And somehow,
I was still holding onto
the broken pieces
left of the promises
you told me.
Although, they were just words to you...
those very same words
were the only thing that
kept the blood flowing
through my veins.

Double edged sword

You promised to help me heal the wounds you created, I accepted that. Not realizing that I shouldn't have these wounds any way.

Bombs of "love"

5

How could you say everything and nothing at
the same time.
How could you see me so clearly, when I was
blind the whole time.

Blindsided

You brought out a side of me, that lived dormant inside of me, a side of me I wish I didn't know existed.

Crash Dummy

You made me question god...
As if, you weren't the test.

Comfort End

asking questions I already know the answer to, knowing you'll try to gaslight me into thinking what I know isn't reality. It's like I became friends with your lies, knowing they'd comfort me when you couldn't.

Numb

I used to want you so badly, but eventually I got tired of waiting for you to keep your word...I just wanted to be free

Cliche

They always say
"If you love it then let it go,"
 but it's real, you should grow.

Repeated cycles

I knew the pain was inevitable
but trying to find the value in every lesson
began feeling like I was searching for something
that wasn't there.

Heated Confessions

12

During every argument
and every word we would end to "regret",
it was only in the heat of these moments
there wasn't one lie said.

still/still?

That the last time,
was the last time,
I thought we moved past this,
healed from this,
so, why does it still hurt?

Wishful thinking

Even after I knew exactly what it was,
 I was hoping one day you could prove me
wrong.

All me

15

How could I fault anyone for not holding an umbrella over my head, as I continued to walk through a storm that wasn't mine to begin with.

Move or be moved

slow dancing with trauma until there was no
more music playing and no one else on the
dance floor
STUCK, mindlessly swaying side to side,
round and round,
complaining about being tired....
 i could've let go at anytime

Twinnnflame

17

It was easy to place blame
blind to my own flaws
seeing my own reflection
right in front of me,
with no mirror in sight

Affordable peace

18

Being so afraid to live in uncomfortable
circumstances, kept me silent.
Trying so hard to keep the peace around me,
leaving me feeling everything but peace within.

lessons learned

19

Sometimes it's easier to love others than
yourself, that doesn't make it right.
You don't have to suffer to prove your solid.

Discernment

Be careful where you plant the seeds, not all soil is capable of producing fruit.